IT CAME FROM THE

MEDIA

RANDY SOUTHERN

VICTOR BOOKS ®

A DIVISION OF SCRIPTURE PRESS PUBLICATIONS INC.
USA CANADA ENGLAND

Other Young Teen Feedback Electives

FAMILY SURVIVAL GUIDE
FOR REAL PEOPLE ONLY
FRIENDS—WHO NEEDS THEM?
NOBODY LIKE ME
THE SCHOOL ZONE
WHAT'S YOUR PROBLEM?
WHEN EVERYONE'S LOOKING AT YOU

Leader's books available for group study

Scripture quotations are from the *Holy Bible, New International Version,* © 1973, 1978, 1984, International Bible Society. Used by permission of Zondervan Bible Publishers.

Cartoons by John Hawk

Library of Congress Catalog Card Number: 89-60171
ISBN: 0-89693-740-2
Recommended Dewey Decimal Classification: 248.83
Suggested Subject Heading: YOUTH—RELIGIOUS LIFE

CONTENTS

AND NOW A WORD FROM OUR AUTHOR...

As the author of *It Came from the Media*, I'd like to give you a short outline of what you *won't* find in this book.

I. All secular rock music is of the devil.
II. Watching too much TV turns your brain to Jello (specifically, lime-flavored).
III. Going to see anything at a theater (other than a Disney cartoon) is immoral.

I'm not going to give you a list of what you should and shouldn't watch or listen to. I figure that choice should be up to you. The decision will mean a lot more if *you* make it for yourself rather than if I try to make it for you.

What I have tried to give you in this book are some biblical principles regarding media issues to help you make your own smart choices. As Christians we have the responsibility to glorify God with everything we do. This includes the things we watch and listen to. I sincerely hope this book helps you develop God-glorifying media habits.

—*Randy Southern*

TUNE-UP TIME

CHAPTER ONE

Bob walked down the hallway from the biology lab to algebra class just as he had every day this semester. But today something was different. Today people were actually *noticing* him. And it wasn't just one or two people; it was everybody! It seemed like every person he passed looked twice at him. Holly—the Homecoming Queen—actually stopped in the middle of a conversation and turned around to smile at him!

What's different about me today? Bob wondered. *Why all this attention? Is it my hair? My clothes? What?*

The more people walked by and smiled 7

at him, the more confident Bob became. He enjoyed the attention. He even started saying hi and waving to people he didn't know, just like the popular people do.

Bob felt like the grand marshal of some big parade. Everyone he passed smiled at him. Finally, outside the algebra classroom, he saw his best friend, Neil.

"Hey, Neil," Bob called, rushing to meet his friend, "you wouldn't believe the day I'm having. I think I'm starting to get popular. Everyone seems to be noticing me today. They're all smiling at me."

"Yeah, no wonder," replied Neil, pulling a handkerchief out of his pocket and handing it to Bob. "You've got something really disgusting hanging from your nose."

Ever had that happen to you? Ever discovered when you got home from school that your slip had been showing or your fly had been open all day? It happens to the best of us. Often these things occur because we forget to check ourselves. If Bob had only looked in a mirror, he certainly would have noticed that green globule hanging from his nose. And he would have saved himself a lot of embarrassment.

What about you, right now? Without checking, can you honestly say that you don't have some green globule hanging from your nose? Is your fly open? Is your slip showing? You can't tell unless you take the time to check. (If you need to, go ahead and make sure. I'll wait for you.)

SPIRITUAL GLOBULES

Using this weird (and disgusting) experience of Bob's as an example, let's take a look at our *inner* selves and discover whether we have any "spiritual globules" going unnoticed in our lives. (Don't try to look up *spiritual globule* in your Bible dictionary. I made up the phrase. I can do that. I'm an author.) Spiritual globules are those things in our lives that are obviously out of place but that we're blissfully unaware of.

Spiritual globules can show up in the way we act, the way we talk, the way we dress, you name it. (And for you comedians out there, no—spiritual globules can't be wiped away with a Kleenex.)

THE GROWTH OF GLOBULES

Where do these things come from, and how do they get in our spiritual lives without our knowing about it? There are several ways, but since this section is on rock music, it's only appropriate that we look at how *rock music* can cause spiritual globules.

Do you think that there are certain songs and types of music that, if listened to enough, can begin to affect us? We'd probably all agree that there are at least *some*. But often the effects of this music aren't immediately noticeable.

Now, if your friend Mike suddenly shaved his hair in the shape of a swastika and began carrying a chainsaw to school after listening to the new "Mass Murderers Live" album 168 times in a row, you could probably tell that the music had an effect on him. But in real life the effects are rarely that obvious (thank goodness).

EARLY WARNING SIGNS OF GLOBULES

Often the effects show up in more subtle ways: we may begin to treat our parents with less respect; we may start swearing or using crude language; we may start lowering our values and morals; we may begin to be rebellious or sullen. Nothing psychotic, but still dangerous.

What about you and the music you listen to? Is it creating any spiritual globules in your life? If you say no, do you know that for a fact? (Remember, Bob walked all the way down the hall thinking nothing was wrong.) One problem with spiritual globules is that we usually don't know when we have them.

RECOGNIZING GLOBULES

The fact is, there are only two ways to know for sure whether or not the music you listen to is causing a spiritual globule in your life. The first is to examine yourself and the music you listen to in light of Scripture. Try to look at yourself as others see you. Do your words, actions, and attitudes honor God? What about the lyrics and subject matter of the songs you listen to? Be honest here. Trying to convince yourself that the globules aren't there when they really are is like looking in a funhouse mirror—you get a distorted image of yourself.

That's why the second way is important. The second way to know if you have any spiritual globules in your life is to ask somebody. Bob needed Neil to point out the foreign substance hanging from his nose. In the same way we need others to point out the things in our spiritual lives that we may not be aware of. There are three good sources to go to for an examination.

● PARENTS—If you're really serious about cleaning up spiritual globules, sit your parents down and say, "Mom and Dad, I'm trying to find out if the music

I'm listening to is causing any problems in my spiritual life. Have you noticed any change in my attitude or behavior that might make you think so?"

"What?!" you're probably saying. "Give my parents a chance to criticize me? They'd tear me to shreds!"

Chances are they won't. If your parents are Christians and they know you really want to become a stronger Christian, they'll probably be glad to help you. If they're not Christians, they'll most likely be pleased that your faith at least makes you want to be responsible at home. But even if they pull out a legal pad and begin numbering one to a hundred, listen to what they say.

● YOUTH PASTOR—If, for some reason, you really can't ask your parents, sit down with your youth pastor and have him or her point out some things about your spiritual life.

● YOUR MATURE CHRISTIAN FRIENDS—If you're not comfortable asking your youth pastor or parents, find a mature Christian friend whose opinion you trust. Make sure this person can look at you objectively and tell you the truth. For instance, if Mike the Swastika Head tells you there's nothing wrong with you, you might want to get a second opinion.

ELIMINATING GLOBULES

Once you've gotten the feedback you need from others, you face the biggest challenge of all: removing the globules. Do you really want to walk around with a spiritual globule in your life? Don't think it's not being noticed by other people, because it is (just as much as other people noticed Bob). More important, it's being noticed by Christ.

So what can you do? Well, first you have to determine specifically what is causing the globule. If you think some of the music you listen to just *might* be negatively affecting you, evaluate it seriously. (We'll talk more about *how* to evaluate your music in chapter 3.)

Be honest with yourself. No matter how much you like the group, or the beat, or the lyrics, if you realize that a certain song or type of music is creating spiritual globules in your life, stop listening to it. That's the second step. Just don't listen to it anymore. It's that simple.

The third and final step is to go back to the people you talked with, thank them for their help, explain that you've eliminated the source of your globule, and let them share your happiness in being back on track. (After all, they cared enough to be honest with you.)

I realize these steps are harder than they sound, but look at it this way: are a few rock songs worth separation from God and others? Answer this question for yourself, then determine what you're going to do.

Oh, and before we end this chapter, Bob sends along this message: Always carry a handkerchief and check your nose.

EVER BEEN CALLED A STUMBLING BLOCK?

CHAPTER TWO

7:55 Tuesday morning. History classroom.

RON: *[Walks in sleepily, sits down, and whispers to Dan, the guy next to him]* If Mr. Pfaff says anything important, like what's gonna be on the test, wake me up.

DAN: What's the matter with you?

RON: The Springsteen concert ended late last night and I didn't get to bed until after midnight. I'm beat.

DAN: You went to the Springsteen concert?

RON: Yeah, it was great. He did three encores.

DAN: I thought you were a Christian.

RON: I am. What does that have to do with it?

DAN: I'm a Christian, and I believe that it's wrong to go to secular concerts and listen to secular music.

RON: Look, it's not like I got drunk or did drugs at the concert. I just went because I like Springsteen's music. What's wrong with that?

DAN: I believe that secular rock music is of the devil.

RON: Yeah? Well I believe that you're a fanatic. So why don't you just drop the subject and wake me up if Mr. Pfaff says anything about the test, OK?

[Dan starts to question again, but Mr. Pfaff's command to "open your books to page 171" interrupts him. Ron puts his head down on his desk, and Dan looks away, confused.]

17

Whose opinion do you agree with—Ron's or Dan's? Do you think it's OK to listen to most secular rock and go to secular concerts (within reason)? Or do you believe that listening to secular rock goes against our Christian beliefs?

TORN BETWEEN TWO PHILOSOPHIES

Let's look at Ron's situation. Let's say that Ron has carefully thought about the music he listens to. He knows that some Springsteen songs aren't necessarily God-honoring. So he skips those songs on his CD and concentrates on those that are positive. He got his parents' permission to go to the concert with his older brother, and although he saw a lot of drinking going on there, he didn't do anything wrong himself. As far as he's concerned, he hasn't done anything to compromise his Christian beliefs.

And yet here's Dan, a new Christian, who believes that listening to secular music and especially going to a secular concert goes against Christian principles. He is confused and offended to learn that Ron can listen to Springsteen's music, go to a Springsteen concert, and still call himself a Christian.

Ron seems to be making mature, responsible decisions about the music he listens to. Assuming he doesn't have any of the "spiritual globules" we talked about in chapter 1, would you say that Ron needs to worry about what Dan thinks?

Let's look at what the Bible says.

● **Make up your mind not to put any stumbling block or obstacle in your brother's way (Romans 14:13).**

What are you saying—that Ron is putting a stumbling block in Dan's way? 19

- **Love your neighbor as yourself (Mark 12:31).**

Yeah, so what does that have to do with this situation?

- **Whoever loves his brother lives in the light, and there is nothing in him to make him stumble (1 John 2:10).**

Then was Ron wrong in telling Dan that he went to a Springsteen concert? What do you think?

DON'T BE A STUMBLING BLOCK

Unless we come up with some dramatic new interpretation of these passages, it's obvious that we have a responsibility to live our lives so that we don't become "stumbling blocks" to other Christians.

A stumbling block is any action that could give somebody the wrong idea about Christianity. Even if *we* believe it's OK to do something, we need to be sure that what we're doing won't make anyone question our faith or God's goodness.

You see, as Christians, we're all part of the body of Christ. In a sense, we're all on a team. And when we cause another Christian to stumble by confusing him or her with our actions, it's a lot like someone on a football team tackling one of his teammates. The whole team suffers.

SOLUTIONS

What's the solution? Should all Christians listen to the exact same music so no one gets offended or confused? Of course not. There are a lot of better ways to handle it. (Besides, I'd be afraid that we'd all have to listen to disco.) Try this three-step approach.

● First, make absolutely certain that what you're listening to isn't displeasing to God. Don't fool yourself. Examine the songs you listen to closely. (We'll get very specific about how to do that in chapter 3.)

• Second, when you've made sure that your songs are OK, if you think that someone may get the wrong idea about your musical freedom, keep your musical freedom to yourself. If you like heavy metal and have found some non-offensive songs to listen to, there's no need to go flaunting yourself as a metalhead. Keep it to yourself. Enjoy it on your own. (But don't lie about it. If someone questions you, move to step three.)

• Third, always be ready with an explanation when someone challenges you about your music. Ideally you should be able to show the person exactly why you believe a song is not dishonoring to God. (You should be able to do this with every song you listen to.) Then be sure to ask the person for his or her opinion. If you have a good enough reason for listening to your music, he or she won't be able to object. But if the other person has a good enough argument *against* your music, you might want to reconsider listening to it. Always be willing to change your listening habits to avoid being a stumbling block—to Christians and non-Christians alike.

And don't go tackling your teammates.

MUSICAL ROBOTS

CHAPTER THREE

When Julie saw the ad proclaiming, "Learn to Control Your Friends through Mind Power!" in the back of *16½ Magazine*, she didn't really believe that mind control would work. But she was feeling weird that day, so she sent away for it.

Six weeks later when she received the "Mind Power" booklet, she was still skeptical. But since she'd shelled out $4.95 for the thing, she figured she might as well try it.

Stare deep into your victim's eyes, the instructions read, *until you see the pupils dilate. When that happens, you have control of the person's mind.*

On the school bus the next day Julie decided to try the method out on her friend Kathy. She figured that, if nothing else, it would be good for a laugh.

"Kathy," she said, "look into my eyes."

"Why—have you got dirt on your contacts again?" asked Kathy.

"No, I just want you to try something. Look into my eyes until I tell you to stop."

"OK," Kathy said gamely.

After a minute and a half of hard staring, Julie noticed Kathy's pupils beginning to dilate.

"Kathy?" Julie asked excitedly.

"Yes?" Kathy replied in a monotonous, trancelike voice.

"Stick your head out the bus window," Julie ordered.

"Yes, ma'am," Kathy replied, sticking her head out the window.

"Now come back in," Julie said.

"Yes, ma'am," Kathy replied, pulling her head in.

Julie couldn't tell if Kathy was just playing along or not, so she decided to try the acid test. "Kathy, go kiss zit-face Brian on the forehead," she ordered. And to her amazement, Kathy did just that—to the surprise and disgust of everyone on the bus (except Brian, who shouted, "Do it again! Do it again!").

At school that day, Julie did the same thing to all her friends. By lunchtime, she had control of over 30 people. All of them were following Julie around (because she'd ordered them to).

This is great, Julie thought.

"Everyone tell me how beautiful I am, what a good friend I am, and how much you love me," she ordered.

Immediately, cries of "I love you, Julie" and "You're beautiful, Julie" and "You're the best friend I've ever had, Julie" rose up.

"Tell me that I'm the most important person in the world," she said, basking in the glory.

"You're the most important person in the world," her friends said.

"Tell me—" Just then Julie's alarm went off and she woke up.

WE'RE NOT ROBOTS

OK, OK; I know it's a stupid story. But it illustrates a point we need to look at. How would you feel if you had the power that Julie had in her dream? What kind of embarrassing things would you have your friends do? It might be fun for a while.

But after a few hours (or days), wouldn't it get boring? Think of it—you could never have any real relationships with people because they would do and say only what you told them. Some life, huh?

Now think of our relationship with God. He could have created us like Julie's friends in her dream: mindless robots who did only what we were told. That way He could have made sure that we would always follow Him. But He didn't. Instead, He created us with two very special features: the ability to reason and a will.

Reasoning is the ability we have to look at a situation, find out everything we need to know about that situation, and then make our decisions about that situation. Human beings are the only creatures to whom God gave the ability to reason.

By creating us with *wills*, God has given us the ability to do as we please. This includes the freedom to choose between right and wrong.

How does it make you feel to know that God has given you such freedom? Excited? A little scared? After all, it's a big responsibility. God *wants* us to use our wills and reasoning abilities to honor Him, but because He's not *making* us do anything, we can (and often do) blow it.

SO WHAT?

At this point you may be saying, "All this is interesting—but I thought this session was about rock music. What does this stuff have to do with rock music?

Good question. Think about it this way. Do you ever hear a song and automatically start singing along with it just because it has a good beat or because you like the group that sings it? Do you ever listen to a song without paying attention to the words? I do.

Can you see how we're sometimes like robots in our music habits? After all, we have the reasoning ability to examine the song and the will to accept or reject it. So if we just sit there and listen to a song without thinking about what it says,

we are wasting two of God's great gifts
to us.

GLORIFYING GOD

"So whether you eat or drink or whatever you do, do it all for the glory of God" (1 Corinthians 10:31).

Notice it doesn't say, "If you're paying attention to it, do it for the glory of God," but *whatever* you do, do it for the glory of God." Everything. It's our responsibility to make sure that our listening habits *always* glorify God.

How do we do that? Find out what we're hearing. Know the lyrics to the songs we listen to. Look at what the words are saying. Pay attention. If you can't understand a song, don't listen to it. Better safe than sorry.

What does it mean to glorify God? Obviously not every song is going to mention God in its lyrics. But a song doesn't have to mention God or the Bible to be God-glorifying. Many songs celebrate emotions and relationships that are God-given. For instance, how many songs do you know that talk about love? Love is a gift from God. Therefore, a "good" love song could glorify God (as long as it agrees with what God's Word says about love).

Of course, if you're going to make sure a song agrees with God's Word, you need to know what God's Word actually says. If you don't know, maybe some good Bible study is your first step. Then you'll know what standards to use. In the case of a love song, you could ask:

● Does the song *celebrate* God's gift of love?

● Does its description of love tie in with 1 Corinthians 13?

● Does the song recognize sex as something to be saved for marriage?

There are many possibilities for examining the music you listen to. You could could get together and examine lyrics with your friends. Or you could do something with it in your personal devotions by picking out a particular song and comparing its lyrics and message with what God's Word says.

Be sure to keep a journal and list every song you determine is OK and every song you determine isn't. Then make a conscious effort to listen to only those songs you've OK'ed.

This sounds like a lot of work, and it is. With God's gifts of reason and will also comes a great responsibility. But won't it be worth it to know that you "do all for the glory of God"?

(Besides, it could be worse. What if the Bible said the only music we could listen to was the Bee Gees and Barry Manilow?)

MY HEROES HAVE ALWAYS BEEN ROCK STARS

CHAPTER FOUR

Stan is a little weird. He loves to watch professional basketball. As a matter of fact, you could call him an NBA fanatic. But while most people go to games to cheer for Michael Jordan's aerial acrobatics or Larry Bird's long-range jump shots or Isiah Thomas' amazing ball-handling, Stan goes to cheer for . . . the referees.

In the stands, he's the only person who gives a standing ovation when the refs are announced. He goes crazy any time a foul is called—on either team. Often he wears a black-and-white striped shirt to show his support. He has an auto-graphed picture of every ref in the league. And when he's really wound up, Stan often tries to start a "Blow that whistle!" chant in the crowd. People look at him like he's crazy, but Stan doesn't care. He wants the whole world to know he's a referee fanatic.

Stan really is a weirdo. With all the incredible basketball players to watch, he chooses referees as his heroes. Stan misses the whole point.

THE STUNNING ANALOGY

Before we criticize Stan too much, let's ask ourselves who our heroes are. Who do you admire? Imitate? Look up to? Whose posters do you have hanging on your wall? Whose pictures or logos do you have on your T-shirts? Think about it and decide who your heroes are.

If you're like most people, you probably thought of a rock star or actor or sports star. With that person (or persons) in mind, think about the following account. (You may have heard or read about it hundreds of times, but rather than just *reading* it this time, *think* hard about it.)

God created us. In His infinite wisdom and power, He created us. He created us so we could have a relationship with Him. How does it make you feel to know that you were created to have a relationship with God?

When God created us, He didn't want us to be robots who automatically did whatever He said just because He said it. So He gave us a will and the ability to reason. And we screwed it up. He gave us a choice to obey Him and we chose sin instead. Imagine for a second that you're God. You've created a race of beings that you love, given them a will, and what do they do? They turn their backs on you and pursue sin. How would you feel? Disappointed? Hurt? Angry? What would you do?

Of course you know what God did. He knew that our sin had caused a split in our relationship with Him. That split meant *eternal* separation from Him. But He loved us so much that He did the only thing that could mend the split. He sent His Son to save us.

So to rescue a headstrong group of rebellious sinners who had turned their backs on God, the infinite Son of God took on human form and lived with us. In the short time He was on this earth He performed miracles the likes of which have not been seen since. He healed sickness, cured deafness and blindness, and even raised people from the dead. In 33 years He changed the course of history.

But that's not all. Jesus Christ did something else. He allowed human beings, the creatures He Himself had created, to put Him to death in the most excruciating manner ever devised—crucifixion.

Because of our sins, He allowed Himself to be beaten, mocked, tortured, blasphemed, and nailed to a cross. He took upon Himself our sin and paid the price for us. He laid down His life so that our relationship with God could be restored.

And He saved the best for last. Because after giving His life for us, Jesus performed His greatest feat yet: He conquered death itself. After being dead for three days, Jesus rose again. In doing this, He created a way for us to have eternal life. Now all we have to do to be assured of eternal life in the unfathomable splendor of heaven is accept Christ as Saviour.

Jesus Christ did all that for us because He loves us.

Now think again about the person (or persons) you chose earlier as heroes.

How do they stack up in the hero department with the Person you've just read about? Jesus kind of makes everyone else look worthless in comparison, doesn't He? Is it possible that, like Stan at the basketball game, you're focusing on second best? Think about this for a moment.

WHAT TO DO WITH A NON-HERO

What should we do then? Tear down our posters, get rid of our T-shirts, and start hanging pictures of Jesus around the house?

That choice is up to you. But here are some principles to remember about this hero business.

● Rock stars (and actors and sports stars) are human beings just like you and me. And they are no more special than we are.

• Any talent or beauty that a rock star has is a gift from God. If someone can play a guitar well, or write great songs, or sing well, or just plain look good, it's because God gave that talent or beauty. So ultimately if you appreciate something about someone, it's God who should be praised. There's nothing wrong with appreciating someone's talent if you keep it in the proper context.

• If you find yourself too wrapped up in a particular person or group, take a step back and compare what you like about them with what you like about Christ. Anyone you compare with Christ will pale in the comparison. This will help you keep a proper focus in your hero worship.

But the choice is yours about what to do with all those badges, posters, stickers, and T-shirts. (If you want to act like Stan, that's your business.)

DON'T PEEK

CHAPTER FIVE

Remember the movie *Ghostbusters*? There's a scene toward the end of the film in which the ghostbusters are told by the evil spirit they're battling to choose the form of the creature that will destroy the earth. In other words, whatever they think of, that's the form the destructor will take. So to prevent this destructor from appearing, the ghostbusters determine to clear their minds of any thoughts. (Those of you who've seen the movie know what happens next.)

One of the ghostbusters can't clear his mind. For some reason he thinks of—of all things—the Sta-Puft Marshmallow

Man. (Hey, I didn't write the movie.) At that moment, an enormous Sta-Puft Marshmallow Man begins to destroy New York City—all because one man couldn't control his mind. All he did was *think* of something and it came into existence.

(Believe it or not, I'm going to relate this bizarre movie scene to a biblical principle.)

In His Sermon on the Mount, Jesus told His listeners, "You have heard that it was said, 'Do not commit adultery.' But I tell you that anyone who looks at a woman lustfully has already committed adultery with her in his heart" (Matthew 5:27-28).

Think about it—if you look at a woman lustfully, you've already committed adultery with her. That's heavy stuff. (And, by the way, ladies, you're not off the hook. This also refers to lusting after guys as well.) What do you think? Isn't it a lot like a ghostbuster creating a Sta-Puft Marshmallow Man just by thinking about it? We create adultery simply by looking at someone lustfully. (OK, so maybe it isn't *a lot* like it, but at least I kept your attention.)

SCREEN LUST

When was the last time you saw something in a movie or on TV that caused you to lust after someone on screen? Last week? Yesterday? Five minutes ago? Unfortunately we live in a society that pushes sex as a primary means of entertainment.

That's a shame for two reasons: one, because, as we just discovered, sexual content which causes us to lust promotes sin; and two, because sexually suggestive content misuses and distorts one of God's most precious gifts to us.

Why do you think God has such strict rules about sex? Because He's a heavenly spoilsport? Nope. Because He knows how special and fantastic sex is, and He doesn't want us ruining His present before He gives it to us on our wedding night. He doesn't want us looking at some perverted, man-made exploitation of His gift. He wants us to experience the real thing. *That's* why He puts such strict rules on it.

"OK, fine," you may be saying. "I understand that it's all important to God. But what am I supposed to do? After all, sex is all around us. You can't watch anything without seeing some kind of sexual content. What am I supposed to do—avoid it altogether?"

Yes. Jesus didn't say, "If you see *a lot* of sexual content *all the time* and you lust *a lot*, it's adultery." He said, "If you look at a woman lustfully you *have* committed adultery." Just once is all it takes.

I'm not saying that overnight you will be able to eliminate all traces of lust-provoking input from your life. But that should be your goal. And guess what one of the easiest aspects of your life to control is? Your viewing habits. Think about it. You don't have to watch anything you don't want to. (Remember, you have a will and the freedom to say yes or no to anything.)

ANTI-LUST CAMPAIGNS

Some young people just like you have worked out methods to control the sexual content they watch.

- If Liz D. is alone watching TV and sees a situation that causes her to lust, she simply switches channels. Simple, huh? If someone is watching TV with her and a questionable scene comes on, she says something like "Mind if I see what else is on?" If the person objects, or if Liz is in a situation where she doesn't feel comfortable switching channels, Liz just quietly and unobtrusively excuses herself from the room until the scene is over.

- John B., on the other hand, prefers to use his VCR as his censor. He likes to watch videos, so the first thing he does before he rents a movie is find out all he can about how much sexual content is in it. He consults video guides and asks people who have seen the movie. If he rents the movie and discovers a questionable part, he fast-forwards the scene. "With the remote control, it's easy to speed past the sex scenes," he explains. "By now, most of my friends know what I object to, so they don't say much about it. But if someone does, I just say, 'Hey, I'm not into these love scenes. I just want to get back to the plot.' It seems to work."

● Clyde P. prefers to see movies in the theater. Like John, he finds out as much as he can about the movies he sees beforehand from movie reviews and word of mouth. As a general rule, he doesn't go see R-rated movies because he's not 17 yet. But when he turns 17, he'll use the same principles he uses for PG and PG-13 movies. If he sees a scene in the movie he's watching which could cause some problems, he goes out to get a drink of water or popcorn (or Ju-Ju Beans or Junior Mints) and returns when the scene is over. If it's inconvenient for him to leave the theater, Clyde just closes his eyes and thinks about something else until the scene is over.

These three young people are probably a lot like you. They're not religious fanatics who stand up and loudly rebuke others for watching sinful trash. They have their own subtle ways of obeying Jesus' words. (Don't get me wrong—if you want to use situations like these to share your principles with your friends, that's fantastic. By all means, do it. But I just wanted to show you that there are workable ways to handle these potentially sinful situations.)

When you get married, you'll discover what an unbelievable gift God has given us in sex. Until that time, don't spoil the gift for 90 seconds of cheap thrills at a time.

IT'S NOT LIKE IT'S REAL BLOOD AND GUTS

CHAPTER SIX

"And the Lord said to Moses, 'Thou shalt not turn thine eye to violence. If thou seest a man killing another, thou shalt turn thine eyes from it. Look not upon any violence, but set thine eyes upon pleasurable things'" (Leviticus 27:35).

How many times have you heard this verse used to argue against violence on TV and in the movies? If you have your Bibles handy, take a moment now and look up Leviticus 27:35. I'll wait for you.

OK, you caught me. I made the verse up. But think about it for a moment. What if God really did set down exact guidelines about how much violence we should watch in the media? Wouldn't it make things a lot easier for us? We wouldn't have to wonder about whether a show or movie was too violent or not; we could just flip to the appropriate section of the Bible and know for sure.

But unfortunately (or fortunately, depending on how you look at it), God makes no mention of media violence anywhere in the Bible. Like many other things, God leaves the specifics of choosing what to watch and what not to watch to us. It's our responsibility.

THREE MODELS

How do you feel about violence in the media? Look at the three following examples of different attitudes toward screen violence and determine which person's views you most closely identify with.

● SUE—Sue is not a fan of screen violence at all. She despises it. She gets upset if characters even start talking angrily in a movie. She thought *The Sound of Music* was too violent. Anything more abrupt than a yawn causes her to jump out of her seat. She believes that all violence should be banned from the screen and that every TV show and movie should be as harmless as "The Lawrence Welk Show."

● DAVE—Dave is Sue's exact opposite. Dave lives for screen violence. He often wears a T-shirt that says, "If it ain't got blood and guts, it ain't a movie." He thinks Rambo is a wimp and prefers really gory movies. He's seen *Texas Chainsaw Massacre* and *Texas Chainsaw Massacre II* 47 times *each.* He has a poster of Freddy Kruger next to his bed and is starting a machete collection. Sometimes if he's feeling really scary, he'll wear a hockey mask to the theater. Chance are, Sue and Dave will never go to a movie together.

● JAY—Somewhere in between Sue and Dave is Jay. Jay doesn't mind a certain amount of blood and guts in a movie if it's part of the plot. He doesn't like gory movies just for the sake of gore. He enjoys a good movie, and if that means seeing some blood and guts, it's no big deal. He knows it's just special effects. Unlike Sue, Jay likes to be scared by a movie; but unlike Dave, he doesn't get an unnatural thrill from violence.

How would you compare yourself to these three? On the line below, mark where you're at based on your feelings on screen violence:

SUE   JAY   DAVE

THE GORE FACTOR

I don't know how to break this to you, but there is no perfect way to determine whether you are watching too much violence and gore. But take heart; there are some guidelines you can use.

● The first thing you can do is determine exactly how you feel about violence in the media. You did this earlier when you marked the line. Were you strongly opposed to it? Were you strongly for it? Does it really matter to you that much?

● When you've determined how you feel about screen violence, answer this question: Why do I feel the way I do?

If you're against screen violence—why?
√ Are you frightened by it?
√ Does it stir up violent emotions in you?
√ Have you been convicted by the Holy Spirit about it?

If you're strongly for it—why?
√ Is it a way to nonviolently release your anger and emotion?
√ Are you fascinated by violence and death?

If you're somewhere in the middle—why?

√ Do you like the thrill of being scared, but are uncomfortable with extreme violence?

√ Do you just like all kinds of movies, no matter what's in them?

Know why you believe what you do. Always be ready with an answer for anyone who asks you to defend your beliefs.

● Once you know your motives for believing as you do about screen violence, check to make sure your motives aren't going against biblical principles. For instance, if your motive for not watching screen violence is that your parents won't let you, that's fine. That's biblical—obey your parents. But if your motive is that the Bible clearly states that violent movies are wrong, that's not fine. The Bible doesn't say that.

If your motive for watching violent movies is that you know it's a movie and you enjoy being scared (like on a roller coaster), that's probably OK. You could argue for that. But if your motive is that violent movies help you release anger in a nonviolent way, that's not OK. All anger should be turned over to God.

You can make sure your motives are spiritually correct by asking the Holy Spirit to convict you of any wrong. Then, using a thing known as your conscience, the Holy Spirit can show you how legitimate your motives are.

IN SUMMARY

The key to determining whether violent movies are OK or not is your motive for watching them. As you've been reminded throughout this book, it's important that you be honest with yourself in determining your motives. If you can't be honest with yourself, you're in trouble.

If you're convicted that your motives for watching screen violence aren't biblical and you want to change your viewing habits, look back at the last chapter's solutions for dealing with screen sex. (Look especially at the suggestions of Liz, John, and Clyde.) The same procedures could apply for violent movies.

One final thought on screen violence that is very important to remember: Avoid going to a movie with someone wearing a hockey mask.

15,000 HOURS
CHAPTER SEVEN

How long do you think it took Eddie Van Halen to learn to play the guitar? How long do you think it took Elton John to learn to play the piano? How long do you think it took Phil Collins to learn to play the drums?

Ever listen to those guys and say, "I wish I could play music like that"? You could.

What is it about Eddie Van Halen, Elton John, and Phil Collins that make them such great musicians? Were they just naturally gifted from birth to make incredible music? No. They worked at it. They practiced. They took the *time* to become great.

That's what it really takes, you know. Becoming a great musician (or becoming a great anything) takes practice, spending the time.

What about you? What is it you want to become great at? Music? Art? Dance? Acting? Sports? Writing? Do you have the time to become great?

How much time do you spend each day watching television? An hour? Two hours? Three? More? (The title of this chapter refers to a study that showed that the average person, by the time he or she graduates from high school, has watched over 15,000 hours of TV. *Fifteen thousand* hours!)

THE GREAT TIME ROBBER

Don't worry. This isn't going to be one of those "TV is rotting your brain" chapters. I don't believe that watching too much TV makes you an evil person. But I do believe that we need to examine our TV-watching habits.

If most people were asked, "Why do you watch TV?" they would probably say something like "Because it's entertaining" or "Because it relaxes me" or "Because there's nothing else to do." All these are understandable responses.

TV *is* entertaining; after a hard day at school, it *is* nice to come home and put our feet up in front of the tube and veg out; when we're bored TV *does* seem like a perfect solution.

But we also need to answer this question: Other than enjoyment, what do we get from TV? If we're honest, the answer is not much. (If you said you watch it for educational purposes—get out of here.) Let's face it, TV is the junk food of all recreational activities.

TV can also be addictive. How many times have you sat down "just to see what was on" and ended up watching TV for three hours or more? It happens to all of us. For some reason, reruns of "Gilligan's Island," "I Dream of Jeannie," and "Leave It to Beaver" have a mesmerizing effect on us.

TIME WELL SPENT

What if you took the time you spend watching TV and started working on becoming great at something?

How much time did you say you spend watching TV each day? For the sake of a round number, let's say you spend 4 hours a day in front of the tube. What if you cut that amount of time in half and watched only 2 hours a day? Then you could use the other 2 hours to practice whatever it is you want to become great at.

Two hours a day figures out to 730 hours a year. Imagine how good a guitarist (or baseball player, or writer, etc.) you could become if you practiced 730 hours a year at it!

GET PICKY

The key to cutting down your TV time is to be selective in what you watch. Pick out one or two shows each day that you *really* want to watch. When it's time for them, watch them. When they're finished, turn off the TV and leave the room (unless someone else is watching TV, of course—then just leave the room). Don't get suckered into sitting through Ginsu knife commercials and old "My Three Sons" episodes just to "see what else is on." Take charge of your TV habits. Control them; don't let them control you.

LAST AND MOST IMPORTANT

If you're not convinced yet that TV watching is something that needs to be controlled, or if you can't think of anything in particular that you want to become great at, I have one more piece of evidence that will be hard to argue with.

Compare the time you spend watching TV with the time you spend in God's Word. How close are the amounts of time? If you're like most of us, they're probably pretty far apart.

It's not as easy to sit down and read the Bible as it is to watch TV, is it? Do you think there's something wrong with that?

Consider this: God tells us to have no other gods before Him (Exodus 20:3). A god doesn't have to be something we bow down to and worship; it can be anything that takes a higher priority than God and His Word.

How about you? Has TV become a god in your life? Do you ever find yourself falling into bed after the late-night movie too tired to pray or read your Bible?

Do the characters of your favorite show sometime seem more real than God does? Do you arrange your schedule according to the *TV Guide* but can't seem to arrange your life according to God's Word?

If so, do something about it. Stop watching so much TV and start spending more time in God's Word. That's not to say that you have to spend *exactly* as much time reading the Bible as you do watching TV, and then everything will be OK. But making a conscientious effort to make God's Word *the* high priority in your life is a step in the right direction. Why not become great at studying God's Word?

All it takes is time.

TWO HEADS ARE BETTER THAN ONE

CHAPTER EIGHT

Pam is one of the best volleyball players in the state of Illinois. She has a wicked overhand serve that is almost impossible to return. Her sets are almost always perfect. And she spikes with a vengeance. There's not much Pam can't do on a volleyball court.

Lisa is one of the best female basketball players in the state of Minnesota. At 5'10", she's able to battle well for rebounds. She shoots 85% from the free throw line. She's an amazingly good ball handler and has a beautiful jump shot. She's quite a ball player.

Steve is one of the best baseball players

in the state of Colorado. On the mound, he has a 92 m.p.h. fastball. He's also an outstanding hitter and fielder. He has great speed and knows the game well. He could probably play professional ball someday.

Yet Pam, Lisa, and Steve have never won a game in their respective sports. Pam's team has never won a volleyball game; Lisa's team has never won a basketball game; Steve's team has never won a baseball game. The reason is simple: Pam, Lisa, and Steve are the only people on their respective teams.

So no matter how well Pam sets up a spike, there's no one there to spike it. And it doesn't matter how well Lisa rebounds, because there's no one to pass the ball to. And it doesn't matter how fast Steve can throw a baseball, because there's no one to catch it. It's tough to be very effective in sports if you're playing by yourself.

THE CHRISTIAN TEAM

In this way, sports and Christianity are a lot alike. It's tough to live the Christian life alone. In fact, Christians need each other even more than ball players need the rest of the team. God says we Christians need each other so much that we're like different parts of one body— Christ's body. "The eye cannot say to the hand, 'I don't need you!' And the head cannot say to the feet, 'I don't need you!' " (1 Corinthians 12:21)

TRYING TO GO SOLO

As you've read this book so far, have you thought of anything you need to change concerning your media habits—whether it be music, movies, or TV? (If you haven't thought of anything, humor me for a few minutes and pretend that you have.)

How do you plan to go about making those changes? Will you make a conscious effort to examine the music you listen to? Will you censor the sexual content you see in movies? Will you cut down on the amount of TV you watch?

All these things are commendable and necessary things to do. But if that's all you're going to do, you might find that you're playing a team sport by yourself.

CHOOSING YOUR TEAM

If you've got all these Christian "teammates" who could help you out, why would you insist on playing alone? (That's not to say that you absolutely can't change your media habits by yourself. Maybe you can. But it would be a lot easier if you had a good team playing with you.)

"Fellowship" is the word Christians use to describe the bond and support we can give one another. Do you have fellowship with other Christians? You probably don't refer to it as "fellowship," but do you have other Christian friends with whom you can share your feelings?

If so, hang on to them. Those friends are God's gift to you. If not, you need to find some.

That's easy for you to say. Where am I supposed to find them?

Good question. The first place to go, obviously, is your church and youth group. Are there any young people there you'd like to get to know? If so, go for it. Make the first move toward a friendship. Start building your team.

If your church isn't the place to go, try a Christian club like Campus Life in your school. This could be a rich source of fellowship for you.

If you have no luck there, check other youth groups in your area. If you are really searching for like-minded Christians, God (the ultimate Coach) will supply your needs and help you build your team.

WORKING TOGETHER AS A TEAM

Once you have a team together, whether it's only 1 or 2 other people or 50, you need to start working together. A good place to start might be your media habits.

As a team, you could begin talking about the shows you watch, the music you listen to, and the amount of time you spend in the media. You could begin to set some general guidelines together.

For instance, Laura might ask her "teammates," "Have any of you seen such-and-such a TV show?" And Seth might say, "Yeah, I watch it a lot. There's some violence in it, but there's usually not much sexual content. It also usually has a good moral to each story. I like it." If no one else in the group disagrees, Laura might decide to watch the show based on Seth's recommendation. That's how Christian teams begin to work together.

That's not to say that everyone in your group has to watch and listen to the exact same things. Think of it more like being "spiritual critics" for each other. Everyone could see the movies and TV shows and listen to the music that he or she likes (as long as it's in line with God's Word) and report to the group on it. If someone sees a movie or show or hears a song that isn't glorifying to God, that could also be reported to the group. That way the rest of the group would know what songs, movies, and TV shows to look (and listen) for and which to avoid. (If you want, you could even keep a list of glorifying and nonglorifying songs, movies, and TV shows.)

Your group should also hold each other accountable to certain standards. For instance, if Marilyn started talking about the Judas Priest song she listened to last night, Kim might say (in a nonthreatening way), "I thought we talked about how bad that song was, Marilyn. Why were you listening to it?"

Kim's not saying, "Hey, Marilyn, you pervert! What are you doing listening to that trash?" She's saying, "Marilyn, you're part of this group, and I care about you. I don't want to see you doing anything to hurt your relationship with God." If Kim and Marilyn are in an accountability group together, not only does Kim have the right to say that to Marilyn, she has the responsibility to.

NO FORMAL DISCUSSION GROUPS

Don't get the wrong idea about these groups. I'm not suggesting that you set aside three hours every Thursday to formally discuss the state of the media in society today (although if you want to, that's fine). These groups are something you could do informally around the lunch table at school or anywhere else for that matter. And it's not like you need an agenda and have a "real" meeting. Someone might start it out by asking, "What did you do last night?" Then someone else might answer, "I watched such-and-such." And someone else might ask, "Was it any good?" That's how discussions get started. Nothing fancy, just regular talk.

Sometimes you may not feel like talking to each other. That's fine—don't. Don't try to force fellowship. Let it develop slowly and naturally. Just make sure that everyone in the group knows that there are others who care about their spiritual well-being.

So if you're not in a support group, stop trying to play the game by yourself. No matter how good you are, you'll be a lot better with a team.

BE A MODEL—
OR LOOK JUST
LIKE ONE
CHAPTER NINE

Jane can't stand the way she looks. According to her, her chest is too flat, her nose is too big, her hair is too frizzy, and her glasses are too thick. In the morning, she has to talk herself into looking in the mirror. She hates everything about herself.

Butch, on the other hand, thinks Jane looks great. To him, everything about her is perfect. She has a great smile, beautiful eyes, and gorgeous curly hair. In Butch's opinion, you'd be hard-pressed to find a better-looking girl than Jane. But Butch would never tell Jane that—because Butch thinks Jane wouldn't look twice at him.

Butch can't stand the way he looks. According to him, he's too tall and too skinny. He has buck teeth and too many freckles. And he's too clumsy when he walks. Butch hates everything about himself.

Kristi, on the other hand, thinks Butch looks great. To her, everything about him is perfect. He's tall and cute, has a great smile, and is very funny. In Kristi's opinion, you'd be hard-pressed to find a better-looking guy than Butch. But Kristi would never tell Butch that—because Kristi thinks Butch wouldn't look twice at her.

Kristi can't stand the way she looks. . . .

THE OUTER SOCIETY

How do you feel about yourself? Are you satisfied with everything about you? If you could change anything about yourself, would you? Of course. We all have something about ourselves that we'd like to change. Why is that?

A lot of this mentality is the result of a society that judges people by their outward appearance—how good they look. And what would you say is the main means of spreading this philosophy of outer beauty? You got it. Your friend and mine—the media.

BEAUTY: SOCIETY'S DEFINITION

Guys, when you think of a "beautiful" girl, what image comes to mind? Do you think of an intelligent, fun-loving, interesting young woman who's a great conversationalist and a good listener? ("Only if she's got a 36-24-36 bod," you may be saying.)

No, usually those personality traits are not the first thing that comes to mind. You start thinking of a *Playboy* model. (I mean, a *Sports Illustrated* swimsuit model. Of course you wouldn't think of a *Playboy* model. . . .) It's the truth, isn't it? That's what society has brainwashed us into believing beauty is.

And girls, when you think of a "handsome" guy (or a stud), what image comes to mind? A caring, sensitive guy who's a lot of fun to be around and who's really concerned about what's going on in your life?

No. You probably think of a Chippendale dancer. (I mean, a hunk from your favorite soap opera.) If so, you're also a victim of media brainwash.

DISCOVERING PERSONAL BEAUTY

Don't worry, you're not going to get a lecture on "It's not what's on the outside that counts; it's what's on the inside" or "Beauty is only skin deep." Because, even though both those statements are true, they really do sound stupid and don't give us much comfort.

Instead, we're going to focus on your personal beauty traits. Do you ever look at a really beautiful girl (by society's definition) or a really handsome guy and ask, "Why couldn't God have made me beautiful?"

He did. God gave you a different kind of beauty. He's given each of us beautiful traits. For some, it's a great body. For others, it's great hair. For others, it's a great complexion. (And there are some people who have all three of these traits.)

But to some of us, God gave different, internal beauty traits. And these traits are every bit as impressive as a great body, great hair, and a great complexion. Some people have the internal trait of a great sense of humor or the ability to listen to others. Others have the gift of compassion or a natural intelligence. Whatever it is, it's God's gift to you, and it's every bit as impressive as external beauty.

DEVELOP, DON'T WISH

It's the nature of the media to cause us to want what we don't have. That is one of the primary tools used by advertisers (which we'll discuss more in chapter 11). If we don't have external beauty, our natural response is to wish we did.

But here's a better solution: rather than wishing for something you don't have, develop those beauty traits that you do have. Developing your personal beauty is a three-stage process: identification, enhancement, and recognition.

● IDENTIFICATION—First you must determine what your personal beauty traits are. When you think of your positive attributes, what are they? What do people compliment you on? In what areas of your life are you comfortable with yourself? These are *your* beauty traits.

● ENHANCEMENT—Once you've identified your personal beauty traits, you need to enhance them and bring them to the forefront of your personality. Just as models enhance their external beauty through exercise and make-up, you can enhance your beauty through practice. For example, if you've identified the ability to listen to others as one of your beauty traits, make a conscious effort to begin using that ability as often as possible.

● RECOGNITION—If you consistently demonstrate your God-given beauty traits, people will begin to recognize them in you. Those people who are attracted to those particular beauty traits will begin to recognize you as a beautiful person.

Just as some people are attracted to externally beautiful girls or handsome guys, others are attracted to internally beautiful people. It may sound corny, but it's true. (I know—I'm one of those guys who is more attracted to a fun-loving girl with a great sense of humor and the ability to listen than a knockout 36-24-36.)

So the choice is yours: worry and complain about not having others' beauty traits, or develop your own.

CONSULT AN EXPERT
CHAPTER TEN

Dear Miss Know-It-All:
I am a 14-year-old girl and I've just met the most fantastic guy ever. He's such a gentleman. He always holds doors for me and walks me home after school each day (carrying my books, of course). He's gorgeous, but he's not stuck up. He's a freshman, and he plays varsity basketball, football, and baseball. He's very smart (4.0 average) and wants to become a brain surgeon. He doesn't believe in sex before marriage, and he's told me he appreciates me for who I am on the inside. He says it doesn't matter to him what I look like on the outside. (I'm a little overweight.) He says that, if it's all right with me, he'd like to stop

seeing other girls so he can spend more time concentrating on me. He says I'm worth giving up everyone else for. But he says I can date as many other people as I want—it won't bother him. He'll wait for me forever, he says. So I need to know—do you think this is a guy I should fall in love and get serious with?

Signed,
Wondering in Wheaton

Dear Wondering:

My advice to you is to dump this jerk as soon as possible. This guy sounds like a real moron. I'm surprised you haven't gotten rid of him sooner. This is the type of guy who, after marriage, will be sitting on a couch in a dirty undershirt and boxer shorts and dark socks watching women's wrestling on TV and ordering you to bring him another beer. I don't know why you need me to tell you to tell this loser to hit the road—it's pretty obvious from what you describe that the guy is a zero with absolutely nothing going for him. Good luck, dear!

Signed,
Miss Know-It-All

ADVICE COLUMNISTS

What do you think of Miss Know-It-All's advice? Kind of makes you want to get her advice for all your problems, huh?

What's your opinion of advice columnists? Have you ever written to one for advice? Do you ever read their columns in the newspaper or in a magazine like *Seventeen* or *Sassy*?

How in the world is it possible for someone to give advice to a person if they've never met? Of course, a lot of advice columnists are trained counselors and know a lot of theories and case studies. And those who give relevant, Bible-based advice are certainly worth listening to. But most advice columnists don't know the specific situations of the individuals writing them. And because of that, sometimes they can give the wrong advice. That's why many people believe that advice columnists can often do more damage than good. Do you agree?

OTHER "ADVICE COLUMNISTS"

Where do you go when you want advice? Your friends? Ann Landers? Self-help guides? How do you know if the advice you're getting is good advice?

Any advice you get that is not biblically based is the wrong advice. And in taking bad advice, you're throwing away a great opportunity for *real* advice.

SAVIOUR AND LORD OF OUR LIVES

When you became a Christian, you accepted Jesus as your Saviour and acknowledged Him as Lord of your life. Think about those phrases "Saviour" and "Lord of your life."

What does it mean to have Jesus as your Saviour? It means that you accept the fact that because of your sin and God's holiness, the only way you can have a relationship with God is through Jesus.

What does it mean to acknowledge Jesus as Lord of your life? It means that not only do you accept what Jesus has done for you as your Saviour, you also turn your entire life over to Him for Him to do with as He sees fit. It is a complete giving of yourself to Him.

PERSONAL ADVICE COLUMNIST

One of the exciting things about having Jesus as Saviour and Lord of your life is that you have someone who cares more deeply than anyone else ever could about every aspect of your life. No matter how small or trivial a problem may be, Jesus cares.

But you don't have just anyone caring about you—you have the all-knowing, all-powerful Son of God caring about you. And He knows much, much more about you and your happiness than anyone else, including yourself. He knows the future and realizes how your choices and actions today will affect it.

And He's ready, willing, and able to help you with your problems, struggles, and sorrows—just ask Him. He's the perfect advice-giver.

COMMUNICATING

Of course, it may seem a bit tough to actually know what Jesus' advice *is* on certain subjects. (After all, He doesn't write a newspaper column.) But if you're really looking for His advice, you'll get it. And you'll know it when you get it. There are several ways Jesus communicates with us.

● THE BIBLE—This is Jesus' primary advice-giving tool. You may be surprised at how many of your problems, doubts, and fears can be solved by applying biblical principles. But first you have to *know* biblical principles. Begin a daily study of God's Word. Don't just "read a chapter a day." Find out what the Bible says about the problems you're facing today. Repeat: You may be surprised at how many problems can be solved by applying biblical principles. (You're not going to find things like "If thy date expects a kiss on the first date, thou shalt dump him." But you will find basic guidelines to follow in that situation.)

● PRAYER—Talk to God directly about your problems—and let Him speak to you. Chances are His answer won't be dramatic—no cloud coming from heaven with a voice like thunder. It may just be a sense of peace about a certain decision or an "open door" in a situation that previously seemed closed.

● MATURE, CHRISTIAN ADULTS— God can use a godly, mature Christian to give you His advice. If you can find someone fitting this description that you trust—maybe a parent or youth leader or pastor or someone else—ask that person for advice. Then listen carefully to make sure it's in line with what you know of biblical principles. If it's in line, take the advice to heart. It's the Lord of your life communicating with you.

(You know, if enough people had Jesus as Lord of their lives, Dear Abby and Ann Landers would be looking for another line of work.)

KEEPING UP WITH THE JONESES

CHAPTER ELEVEN

It's the most incredible day of your life. First you get a phone call from a building contractor. He tells you that you have been selected to design the house of your dreams to be built for free anywhere in the United States. Where would you have your dream house built? What would the house look like? Remember, it's free.

After you've barely recovered from the shock of this phone call, you receive another. It's from your local foreign-car dealer. He tells you that you are the lucky winner of a contest you don't even remember entering. For your prizes, you get any two cars in the world (whether you drive or not). What two kinds of cars would you choose as your prizes?

As soon as you hang up, you get another call from the owner of your local mall. It seems you've won another contest, and the prize for this one is a $50,000 gift certificate to the clothing store of your choice. The gift certificate may not be used for anything except to buy clothes for yourself. Which store would you choose to shop at?

Just then the doorbell rings, and when you answer, a man hands you a telegram informing you that you have won the state lottery with a ticket someone bought in your name last week. Although the grand prize this week is only $9 million, you figure it will keep you going for a while.

You're about ready to faint from excitement when you get one more phone call. On the other end is the one person in this world you would love to date more than anyone else. This person tells you that whether you knew it or not, he (or she) has been in love with you for some time and wonders whether you feel the same way.

NEVER ENOUGH

If all these things happened to you, do you think you'd be content? Would you say that you had everything you need? You know what? You probably wouldn't. It wouldn't be enough.

Of course, most of us would like to try to get along with a new house, two cars, a new $50,000 wardrobe, $9 million cash, and the perfect boyfriend or girlfriend. But soon we'd be wanting something else—a new wing added to our house, another car, more clothes, $10 million, and a better-looking boyfriend or girlfriend.

You see, our society causes us to lose our focus on what we do have and focus instead on what we don't have. (Sound familiar? If not, you were sleeping through chapter 9.) So no matter how much we have, we will always want more.

A NOT-SO-MYSTERIOUS CAUSE

Here's a really tough question: What five-letter word describes the cause of most of our dissatisfaction? (Hint: It begins with an *m* and ends in an *a*.)

If you said anything other than *media*, go back to page 1 and start reading again.

ADVERTISING TRICKS

We discussed earlier how the goal of advertising is to cause us to be dissatisfied with what we have. This could be said of most media.

Do you ever see something on a commercial or in a TV show and say, "Man, I wish I had that"? Of course; we all do. Is there something wrong with that?

WHAT'S THE BIG DEAL?

In biblical terms, this act of wishing we had something we don't is called coveting. In fact, one of the Ten Commandments is "Do not covet."

But be honest; does coveting really sound that horrible? "Do not murder"— that's easy to understand, or "Do not commit adultery." But "Do not covet"? Sounds like kind of a wimpy sin, doesn't it? What's wrong with coveting?

WHO KNOWS MORE—YOU OR GOD?

Well, there are two things wrong with coveting. First, it takes our eyes off what God has given us. If we're always wanting something else, we tend to take for granted what we do have. That's not showing proper gratitude to God.

Second, and worse, is the fact that coveting assumes that we know more about our happiness than God does. If we're saying, "Wow, I'd really be happy if I had that," what we're really saying is, "I know You've given me this, God, and that I should be happy with it. But You're wrong. I'd be more happy with something else."

We really have no idea what will make us happy. Only God knows. He knows the future and how our actions today will affect it. So the best thing we can do is trust Him and His wisdom. He'll supply our happiness.

But if you think you know more than God, go ahead—covet.

EVERYTHING YOU ALWAYS WANTED IN A BEER....

CHAPTER TWELVE

All right. Here's a quiz for you media experts out there. Finish the following advertising slogans and then name the product being advertised.

1. "Everything you always wanted in a beer ___ ___."
2. "It doesn't get any ___ ___ ___."
3. "Please don't ___ the Charmin."
4. "Listen to the ___ of America."
5. It's a good time for the ___ ___ of McDonald's."
6. "When you care enough to send ___ ___ ___ ___."
7. "It takes a licking and ___ ___ ___."
8. "Good to the last ___."

9. "Just for the ___ of it."
10. "There's a real party animal, his name is ___ ___."

ANSWERS
1. and less (Miller Lite beer)
2. better than this (Old Milwaukee beer)
3. squeeze (Charmin bathroom tissue)
4. heartbeat (Chevrolet)
5. great taste (McDonald's)
6. the very best (Hallmark cards)
7. keeps on ticking (Timex watches)
8. drop (Maxwell House coffee)
9. taste (Diet Coke)
10. Spuds McKenzie (Bud Light beer)

So how did you do? If you're like most of us who've watched a lot of TV, you probably got at least 7 right. And I'm sure there are many of you who got all 10 with no problem.

FREQUENCY = FAMILIARITY

How do you do it? How is it that you know so many ads? Do you sit down in front of the TV and say, "OK, today I'm going to memorize the Miller Lite slogan and the Charmin bathroom tissue slogan"?

Of course not. (If you do, I would strongly suggest that you find yourself a hobby. You sound like a very bored person.) We learn these slogans because of the frequency with which we see them.

If we see a certain commercial twice a day—and many of them we see a lot more than twice—that means we're seeing the commercial at least 14 times a week. If we see and hear *anything* 14 times a week, it's going to stay with us.

BILLIONS OF DOLLARS

Do you know that many of the ads you see on TV are aimed at you? Not your parents, not other adults—you, the young person. Advertisers know how much TV you watch, so they make commercials that will appeal to you.

As a matter of fact, they spend billions of dollars making commercials that will appeal to you. *Billions of dollars.* How does it make you feel to know that your opinion is worth billions of dollars?

YOU, THE CONSUMER

Advertisers use this money as an investment. They know that if you're not already making decisions about how you spend your money, you soon will be. And they want that money spent on *their* products.

So they make the commercials that appeal to you now, knowing their products will be fresh in your memory when it comes time to spend your money. Makes sense, huh? They spend money now to get more money back later.

"Wait a minute," you may be saying. "Just because I know an advertising slogan doesn't mean I'm going to go run out and buy that product." Well, that's true—in a way. Of course it's not a direct cause-and-effect kind of thing. But the fact is that we do tend to buy the products we're most familiar with. And we become familiar with products through advertisements. So, as hard as it may be to admit, our continuous exposure to advertising does have an effect on us. (It had better, if there are billions of dollars at stake.)

NOT OF THE DEVIL

No, I'm not going to tell you that advertising is of the devil and that if you allow it to affect you, you're doomed. The fact is that advertising can be helpful. We *need* to know about products before we buy them.

The key to dealing with advertising is to take away its power. Use it for *your* benefit to become a more informed consumer. Don't be used for its purposes. Recognize that every ad you see is trying to influence you. Don't let it. Take control of your viewing (and buying) habits. Don't be controlled.

A BIBLICAL APPLICATION

Let's look at a more important issue concerning this issue of exposure and familiarity. If merely sitting in front of a TV and being exposed to ads can cause us to remember and be affected by them, couldn't the same principles apply to our spiritual lives?

What if you spent just an hour a day (using one of the hours you cut from you TV viewing time in chapter 7) reading the Bible and praying? That comes out to seven hours a week. If you're exposed to something for seven hours a week, it won't be long before that something begins to affect you.

God's goal for us as Christians is that we be Christlike. (Just like the goal of advertisers is that we buy their products.) One of God's means for making us Christlike is His Word. (Advertisers' means for getting us to buy their products is advertising.) Constant exposure to God's Word is one way we become

Christlike. (Constant exposure to advertising is how we end up buying certain products.)

If God achieves His goal for us and we become Christlike, we get eternal happiness and fellowship with Him. (If advertiser achieve their goals for us, we get a roll of bathroom tissue, or something equally important.)

Expose yourself to God's Word. Make sure you're reading it every day. Let it gradually become absorbed into your subconscious. Let it begin to affect your decision-making. Make it a part of your life.

You have my solemn word that the results will be infinitely more valuable than a roll of bathroom tissue.